SEA LIFE

# ORCAS

by **Elizabeth R. Johnson**

raintree

a Capstone company — publishers for children

Raintree is an imprint of Capstone Global Library Limited, a company incorporated in England and Wales having its registered office at 264 Banbury Road, Oxford, OX2 7DY – Registered company number: 6695582

www.raintree.co.uk
myorders@raintree.co.uk

ISBN 978 1 4747 2588 0 (hardback)
20  19  18  17  16
10 9 8 7 6 5 4 3 2 1

ISBN 978 1 4747 2592 7 (paperback)
21  20  19  18  17
10 9 8 7 6 5 4 3 2 1

**British Library Cataloguing in Publication Data**
A full catalogue record for this book is available from the British Library.

**Editorial Credits**
Jaclyn Jaycox, editor; Philippa Jenkins, designer;
Svetlana Zhurkin, media researcher; Gene Bentdahl, production specialist

**Photo Credits**
iStockphoto: CostinT, 13, Lazareva, 7, Serega, 17; Newscom: VWPics/Francois Gohier, 15, VWPics/Gerard Lacz, cover, 19, 21; Shutterstock: Mike Price, 3, Miles Away Photography, 11, Monika Wieland, 9, Tory Kallman, 5, Triduza Studio, back cover, 6, 12, 16, 24

Design Elements by Shutterstock

Printed and bound in China.

# Contents

# Life in the ocean

A black and white orca splashes through the waves. Orcas are also called killer whales. They are the largest type of dolphin.

Orcas live in oceans around the world. They spend their whole lives in family groups called pods.

# Up close

An orca's black and white skin acts as camouflage. Orcas are about 7 metres (22 feet) long. They can weigh as much as 5 tonnes.

An orca has flukes and flippers.

They help an orca to swim.

An orca also has a tall

dorsal fin.

dorsal fin

flippers

flukes

Orcas love to make noise!

Each pod sounds unique.

An orca can hear its pod

from several kilometres away.

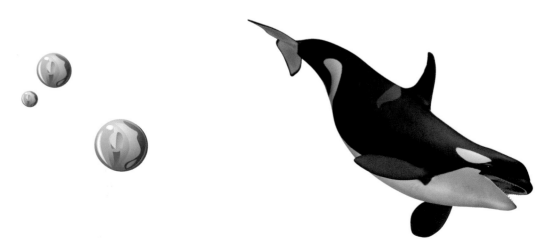

# Finding food

Orcas are one of the world's top predators. Each pod hunts as a team. Orcas eat sea lions and fish. Some pods even hunt sharks and blue whales!

Orcas have about 50 teeth.

The teeth are shaped like cones.

Orcas use their big teeth to

bite and tear prey.

# Life cycle

A baby orca is called a
calf. A newborn calf can be
2.6 metres (8.5 feet) long.
The calf weighs almost
180 kilograms (400 pounds).

Many calves live with their
mothers for their whole lives.
The calves learn how to hunt
and stay safe. Orcas live for
about 50 years.

# Glossary

**calf**  young orca

**camouflage**  pattern or colour on an animal's skin that helps it to blend in with the things around it

**dorsal fin**  fin on the back of a dolphin or whale

**flipper**  one of the broad, flat limbs of a dolphin or whale that helps it to swim

**fluke**  part of the tail of a whale or dolphin

**pod**  group of whales; pods range from fewer than five whales to more than 30 whales

**predator**  animal that hunts other animals for food; killer whales are top predators because no animals hunt them for food

**prey**  animal hunted by another animal for food

**unique**  one of a kind

# Read more

*Animals that Hunt* (Adapted to Survive), Angela Royston (Raintree, 2014)

*Orcas* (Animal Abilities), Anna Claybourne (Raintree, 2014)

*Whales and Dolphins* (Usborne Discovery), Susanna Davidson (Usborne Publishing, 2008)

# Websites

**www.bbc.co.uk/nature/life/Killer_whale**
Learn more about killer whales.

**www.bbc.co.uk/nature/life/Cetacea**
Discover more about whales, dolphins and porpoises.

# Index